Vorwort

Liebe Englisch-Lerner und Praktiker,

Das Übungsheft zur *Communication Expert Grammatik* richtet sich an Englischlerner, die ihr Grammatikwissen praxisorientiert auffrischen und handlungsorientiert trainieren wollen. Es bietet den Vorteil, dass die Übungen durchgehend an berufliche Situationen geknüpft sind und Sie somit die richtige englische Grammatik situationsbedingt trainieren.

Das vorliegende Übungsheft enthält – analog zum Grammatikbuch – 14 Kapitel. Grammatik und Übungsheft sind eng miteinander verzahnt: Sie finden im Grammatikbuch Verweise mit Seitenangaben zu den passenden Übungen des Übungshefts.

Lösungsschlüssel zur Selbstkontrolle

Ferner bietet Ihnen das Übungsheft einen **Lösungsschlüssel** zur Selbstkontrolle. Diesen können Sie unter www.klett.de downloaden. Einfach im Suchfeld den **Online-Link** 808208-0001 eingeben.

Online-Test zur Diagnose des Wissensstandes

Am besten absolvieren Sie den Online-Test, bevor Sie sich mit den Übungsaufgaben beschäftigen. Dann können Sie gleich Prioritäten setzen und Ihre Kenntnisse gezielt vertiefen:

- Geben Sie unter www.klett.de im Suchfeld den Zugangscode **808207-1000** ein. Dort finden Sie einen Test, den Sie online absolvieren können.
- Anhand des Testergebnisses sehen Sie auf einen Blick, in welchen Bereichen noch Übungsbedarf besteht. So können Sie die Grammatik individuell nutzen und Ihren persönlichen Wissensstand optimal berücksichtigen.
- Wenn Sie alle benötigten Kapitel bearbeitet haben, empfiehlt es sich, den Online-Test noch einmal durchzuführen. Sie werden feststellen, dass Sie dieses Mal noch besser abgeschnitten haben!

Die *Communication Expert Grammatik* und das vorliegende Übungsheft ermöglichen Ihnen ein selbstständiges und eigenverantwortliches Lernen.

Wir wünschen Ihnen viel Erfolg beim Nachschlagen und Üben!

Inhalt nach grammatischen Strukturen

Vorwort 1

Wortstellung 4

Mehrzahl 5

Personal- und Reflexivpronomen 6

Make vs. do 8

Genitiv 9

Possessivpronomen 10

Zählbare und nicht zählbare Dinge: a lot (of), lots of, much & many 11

Unbestimmte Pronomen: some & any und die Zusammensetzungen von
some, any, every & no 12

Simple present – present progressive – present perfect –
present perfect progressive *(since & for)* 13

Simple past – past progressive *(while & when)* – past perfect –
past perfect progressive 19

Will-future 24

Going to-future 25

Will-future vs. going to-future 26

Zukunftsformen im Überblick 27

Gerundium & Infinitiv 28

Steigerung der Adjektive 30

Adjektive & Adverbien 32

Inhaltsverzeichnis

Steigerung der Adverbien 32

Relativsätze 34

Modalverben 36

If-Sätze, Typ I 38

If-Sätze, Typ II 39

If-Sätze, Typ III 41

Indirekte Rede 43

Passiv 45

Sich korrekt ausdrücken – Expressing yourself correctly

Wortstellung – Word order

1. You want to write an email to Lauren. Form sentences from the information given below. (Remember: subject – verb – object!)

   1. a really cool place / New York / sounds like

   2. my English skills / to improve / I / want

   3. I / something for your parents / to bring / would like

   4. a little nervous / I / about the new school / am

   5. much / hasn't / my English / yet / improve

2. Read this blog entry from Nicole, a German student in New York. Unfortunately she has mixed up the word order. There are seven sentences that need correcting in total. Rewrite the text correctly on a separate sheet of paper.

Happy New Year!!!!
posted by NYC Nikki, *on 01/01/10, 11.28 am*

Happy New Year from the Big Apple! My name is Nicole. I am 18 and from Leipzig. I have been living for the last two months in New York with a host family. I go to a high school here and I love it. Sure, I had in the beginning trouble understanding everybody and I wanted to go home, but I started after a couple of weeks to feel at home. I now have a lot of friends here and we all last night celebrated at Times Square New Year's Eve. There were there around one million people. It was unbelievable! There were at midnight all over the city fireworks, and people cheered and hugged and kissed each other. Unfortunately I am in two weeks flying home ☹. I love New York!

Mehrzahl – Plural forms

3. Write the correct plural form of these nouns.

1. country   _____   7. husband   _____
2. woman   _____   8. potato   _____
3. person   _____   9. company   _____
4. nationality   _____   10. city   _____
5. housewife   _____   11. church   _____
6. celebrity   _____   12. fish   _____

4. Choose either the singular or plural form of the verb. Sometimes both forms are possible.

1. The New York Yankees ☐ is / ☐ are one of the most famous baseball teams in the USA.
2. All of the information you need ☐ is / ☐ are on the Website.
3. The company ☐ is / ☐ are one of the market leaders in MP3 players.
4. Most school children now ☐ has / ☐ have an MP3 player of some kind.
5. ☐ Does / ☐ Do the police in New York all carry guns?
6. My family ☐ is / ☐ are very important to me. We do a lot of things together.
7. My friend went to San Francisco two years ago. She told me the people there ☐ was / ☐ were very friendly.
8. My father works for a small IT company. ☐ It / ☐ They design websites.

5. Lauren has written some information for you in German. Translate them back into English, and watch out for the plural forms!

1. In New York gibt es viele verschiedene Nationalitäten.

   _____

2. Die Polizei hier ist sehr streng. Seit zehn Jahren gibt es viel weniger Verbrechen.

   _____

3. In den USA arbeiten viele Frauen in Führungspositionen.

   _____

4. Die Stadt ist immer voll mit Touristen aus aller Welt.

   _____

5. Viele große Unternehmen haben ihren Hauptsitz in New York.

   _____

6. Meine Freunde sind verrückt nach Promis. Sie halten immer Ausschau!

   _____

Sich mit dem Unternehmen vertraut machen – Getting to know the company

Personal- und Reflexivpronomen – Personal and reflexive pronouns

1. One of Alex's first jobs is to look after the telephones and take messages for his supervisor, when necessary. Use the correct personal pronouns in subject or in object case from the box below to complete Alex's messages.

she	we	them	we	her	it	us	she
us	they	he	~~him~~	you	I	you	he

Mr Fisher phoned. Please phone _him_ (1.) back this afternoon. _____ (2.) says it is important.

Front desk phoned at 11.25 am. There is a parcel for _____ (3.) at reception. Can _____ (4.) pick _____ (5.) up asap?

Call from Mrs Buckley. _____ (6.) is arriving at 5.35 pm in Berlin. Can you pick _____ (7.) up?

The suppliers phoned. _____ (8.) said that _____ (9.) can expect delivery of the new parts on Thursday. If you want to change the order, you should phone _____ (10.) by Tuesday at the latest.

Lisa from marketing phoned. _____ (11.) wants to take me to lunch ☺. _____ (12.) will be back at 2 pm.

A message for _____ (13.) both from Mr Fletcher. _____ (14.) wants to see _____ (15.) before _____ (16.) go home.

2. Enter the correct reflexive pronouns or pronouns in object case to complete this crossword.

Across
1. "Alex, could I speak to _____ for a moment, please?"
3. "Can you send this to Ms Campbell, please? _____ email address is saved under 'contacts'."
5. "Tomorrow's ideas, today. That's _____ motto here at the company."
6. "Over here is the HR department. Talk to _____ if you have any problems with your wages."
9. "Ms Rigby will explain this to you _____ when she arrives."
10. "I find it very difficult to talk about _____ in front of a lot of people."
11. "Good morning everybody. This is Alex. Would you like to introduce _____ to him one by one, please?"

Down
1. "Welcome to the team, Alex. Please make _____ at home."
2. "The sales team are in a meeting at the moment. They will introduce _____ to you afterwards."
4. "I personally think that this product speaks for _____."
5. "We finished the project under budget. We're very proud of _____."
7. "Did he really come up with the initial idea all by _____?"
8. "That's Daniel. Talk to _____ if you have computer problems."

Wer macht was in Ihrer Firma? – Who does what in your company?

Machen & tun – Make vs. do

1. Tick the correct option – *make* or *do* – to complete these sentences in the proper way.

	make	do	
1.			… a coffee in the morning
2.			… progress
3.			… a good job
4.			… a mistake
5.			… somebody happy
6.			… something for a colleague
7.			… an enquiry
8.			… a lot of business overseas
9.			… a complaint
10.			… a good first impression

2. Some employees at *Howard Electronic Solutions* tell you about what they do. Translate the sentences into English.

1. Ich mache Termine für meinen Chef.

   _____

2. Ich mache Anfragen.

   _____

3. Wir machen Geschäfte mit vielen Firmen im Ausland.

   _____

4. Ich mache Forschung im Bereich Elektotechnik.

   _____

5. Ich mache Vorschläge und Pläne.

   _____

6. Ich mache genau, was der Chef mir sagt!

   _____

3. You are currently doing an apprenticeship at *Howard Electronic Solutions*. On a separate sheet of paper, write ten things that you *make* or *do* there.

Über Besitz und Zuständigkeiten sprechen – Talking about property and responsibilities

Genitiv – s-genitive vs. of-genitive

1. **Read a fellow student's report on the visit and fill in the gaps using either apostrophe + s ('s) or apostrophe (').**

Yesterday__ (1.) tour of *Howard Electronic Solutions* given by Gary Williams was very interesting. He showed us the building__ (2.) different departments. It's a big company and Mr Williams__ (3.) office was very big. He answered the group__ (4.) questions and explained the company__ (5.) structure very clearly. After the tour we had lunch in the employees__ (6.) canteen before visiting Mr Williams__ (7.) colleague. His colleague__ (8.) name was Ms Moss. Ms Moss__ (9.) talk was also interesting, but I found Mr Williams__ (10.) better.

2. **Another student has given you their work to correct. Decide whether they should use *'s* or *of* in the following sentences.**

1. I was surprised by the ☐ size of the company / ☐ the company's size.
2. I found the ☐ presentation of Mr Williams / ☐ Mr Williams' presentation very informative.
3. At the ☐ end of the tour / ☐ tour's end, we had a chance to ask some questions.
4. ☐ The stepbrother of Mr Williams / ☐ Mr Williams' stepbrother, Mr Howard, founded the company in 1981.
5. ☐ The staff's fitness studio / ☐ The fitness studio of the staff was fully kitted out.
6. ☐ The head of the marketing department / ☐ The marketing department's head introduced himself to us.

3. **Translate the following sentences into English, paying attention to the genitive forms. Use an extra sheet of paper.**

1. Der Gewinn der Firma steigerte sich letztes Jahr um 5%.
2. Das Fitnessstudio für die Mitarbeiter wurde vor drei Jahren gebaut.
3. Der zweite Teil der Führung wird nach dem Mittagessen beginnen.
4. Das Mittagessen wird in der Mitarbeiterkantine stattfinden.
5. Das ist das Büro meiner Assistentin.
6. Es war der Traum meines Onkels, eines Tages die größte Elektronikfirma in Europa zu besitzen.
7. Alle Maschinen werden am Ende des Tages gereinigt.

Besitzverhältnisse: Possessivpronomen – Property relations: possessive pronouns

4. Some of the employees at *Howard Electronic Solutions* have sent you messages before your visit to the open day. Rewrite the information, using the correct pronouns.

1. "My name is Theresa Mann and I work in the Human Resources department. My job is taking care of payroll and interviewing new applicants. Our department is very interesting and I am looking forward to meeting your class and showing you all around."

Her name is _____

2. "Our names are Joanna, Beate and Martin. We work in the marketing department. Our job is to come up with marketing campaigns for the company and its products. Our work can be stressful but we enjoy it. We can't wait to tell you all about it."

Their names are _____

5. Decide whether you need *it's* or *its* in the sentences below.

1. This is our new conference room. ☐ It's / ☐ Its only been open for two months.
2. ☐ It's / ☐ Its equipped with the latest video conferencing technology.
3. This is our latest product. ☐ It's / ☐ Its very popular because of ☐ it's / ☐ its multiple features.
4. I think ☐ it's / ☐ its design is beautiful. ☐ It's / ☐ Its very elegant.
5. This machine is not running at the moment. ☐ It's / ☐ Its being serviced.
6. This is our coffee machine. ☐ It's / ☐ Its very old but ☐ it's / ☐ its coffee is still drinkable.

Zählbare und nicht zählbare Dinge – Countable and uncountable nouns: a lot (of), lots of, much & many

6. You now have the chance to ask some questions. Decide whether you should use *how many* or *how much*.

   1. _____ employees …?
   2. _____ experience …?
   3. _____ departments …?
   4. _____ customers …?
   5. _____ turnover …?
   6. _____ time …?
   7. _____ competition …?
   8. _____ factories …?
   9. _____ competitors …?
   10. _____ profit …?
   11. _____ products …?
   12. _____ influence …?
   13. _____ countries …?

7. Complete this extract from Mr Williams' presentation using either *a lot (of)*, *much* or *many*.

A lot of people may not know _____ (1.) about our company, and there are _____ (2.) things that I would like to explain to you today. *Howard Electronics Solutions* are a leader in the portable electronics market. Can anybody guess how _____ (3.) products we currently have on the market? We have as _____ (4.) as 120 different devices on sale around the world. Our most advanced models sell for as _____ (5.) as €2000. As I explained earlier, we have _____ (6.) customers in Asia. However, we also have _____ (7.) in North America and here in Europe. I don't want to take up too _____ (8.) time talking, so let's begin the tour, shall we?

Über Besitz und Zuständigkeiten sprechen

Unbestimmte Pronomen – Indefinite pronouns: some & any and the compounds of some, any, every & no

8. Read the dialogues between Mr Williams and three students and tick the correct word.

1. Mr Williams: Are there ☐ some / ☐ any questions?
   Student 1: Are there ☐ some / ☐ any jobs available?
   Mr Williams: I'm afraid there aren't ☐ some / ☐ any at the moment, but there might be ☐ some / ☐ any by the time you leave university.

2. Student 2: Do you offer ☐ some / ☐ any apprenticeships?
   Mr Williams: Yes we do. Would you like me to send you ☐ some / ☐ any information?
   Student 2: Yes, please. I would like to have ☐ something / ☐ anything to look over.
   Mr Williams: Of course, I will speak to ☐ somebody / ☐ anybody in the HR department and ask them to send you ☐ some / ☐ any brochures in the post.

3. Student 3: Do you have ☐ some / ☐ any advice for us?
   Mr Williams: Yes, I do. If you are interested in ☐ something / ☐ anything, go for it. Don't let ☐ somebody / ☐ anybody or ☐ something / ☐ anything get in your way.
   Student 3: Thanks. ☐ Something / ☐ Anything else?
   Mr Williams: Yes. Learn English. It is spoken almost ☐ anywhere / ☐ everywhere in the world.

9. Choose the correct compound of *some, any, every* and *no* to complete phrases from Mr Williams' presentation. You may only use each compound once.

1. You won't see technology this advanced _____ else in Europe.

2. Can _____ at the back hear me?

3. _____ else has seen this yet. You are the first.

4. Soon, this will be available _____ in the world.

5. Can _____ turn on the lights, please?

6. We would be _____ without our research team.

Arbeitsprozesse und laufende Tätigkeiten beschreiben – Describing operating procedures and ongoing activities

Simple present – present progressive – present perfect – present perfect progressive *(since & for)*

1. **Complete the following sentences using the present progressive and your own ideas. Use the example to help you.**

   1. We usually meet in the conference room,
      but today we're meeting in the canteen.
   2. I often work from home,
      but today _____
   3. She generally leaves early on Tuesdays,
      _____
   4. They often work on projects with one another,
      _____
   5. He usually cycles to work,
      _____

2. **Write questions that match with the answers below. Decide whether you need a question word, or simply *do/does*.**

   1. *When do you check your emails* ?
      I check my emails when I arrive in the morning.
   2. _____ ?
      Yes, they always meet here on Thursdays.
   3. _____ ?
      I usually get to the office at around 8 am.
   4. _____ ?
      The office is closed on Saturdays and Sundays.
   5. _____ ?
      No, she doesn't like long presentations.
   6. _____ ?
      I work in the research and development department.

Arbeitsprozesse und laufende Tätigkeiten beschreiben

3. Complete this dialogue between Mr Bryant and Mr Jones. Decide whether to use the simple present or the present progressive.

1. Mr Jones, I _____ here at least once a week and you   come
   always _____ me that everything is on schedule.   tell
   And now you _____ me that there is a delay.   tell
2. Yes, I'm afraid so. The workers _____ currently
   _____. They say that they aren't paid enough.   complain
3. This is not my problem, Mr Jones. Do you _____ how   know
   much money is tied up in this building?
4. Yes, Mr Bryant. You _____ it every time you visit.   mention
5. Well, now I _____ it again. This building   mention
   _____ worth over $140 million. And, at the moment, it   be
   _____ us almost $100,000 for every day the workers   cost
   don't _____!   work
6. What more can I _____, Mr Bryant?   say
   I _____ everything that I can.   do

4. Translate the questions below using the present perfect.

Mr Bryant fragt …

1. ob Mr Jones schon mit den Bauarbeiten gesprochen hat.
   _____ (speak)
2. ob die Bauarbeiter die neuen Bedingungen akzeptiert haben.
   _____ (accept)
3. ob die Bauarbeiten wieder angefangen haben.
   _____ (resume)
4. ob es weitere Verspätungen gegeben hat.
   _____ (be)
5. ob er schon einen neuen Zeitplan gemacht hat.
   _____ (make)
6. ob er den Kunden schon informiert hat.
   _____ (inform)

Arbeitsprozesse und laufende Tätigkeiten beschreiben

5. You report back to Mr Bryant. Use the words below to form your answers in the present perfect.

1. Mr Jones / speak / to the construction workers / already
   _____

2. the construction workers / not accept / the new terms
   _____

3. construction work / not resume / yet
   _____

4. there / be / further delays
   _____

5. Mr Jones / not made / new schedule / yet
   _____

6. he / inform / the customer / already
   _____

6. Read the following texts and decide whether you need *since* or *for*.

1. "I've been on this site _____ three months, almost _____ the project began, in April. The weather's been pretty rough _____ the last couple of weeks so we're a bit behind schedule. Still, when you've been in this business _____ as long as I have, you get used to the occasional delay."

2. "Ok everybody, a lot has happened _____ our last meeting. _____ the last two weeks bad weather has put a stop to all construction work. I haven't heard from our man at the site _____ yesterday, but I've been updating the customer daily _____ the beginning of the week."

3. "I've been working together with your company _____ many years now, but I'm worried about the lack of progress. There has been very little activity _____ I spoke to you last Monday, and absolutely no construction work _____ the beginning of last week. Should I be worried?"

Arbeitsprozesse und laufende Tätigkeiten beschreiben

7. Rewrite the sentences below using either the present perfect or the present perfect progressive and *since* or *for*.

1. The construction workers began striking ten days ago.

   The construction workers have been striking for ten days.

2. The last time we had such a delay in a project was three years ago.

   _____

   _____

3. We began negotiating with the workers five days ago and we're still negotiating.

   _____

   _____

4. The weather started to be bad last weekend, and it is still bad.

   _____

5. I visited the site last week. I did not visit this week.

   _____

6. Mr Bryant started talking with the customer at 9 am. It's now 11 am and he's still on the phone.

   _____

   _____

8. Following your update, Mr Bryant is calling the client to give them an update. Fill in the gaps using either the present perfect or the present perfect progressive.

… Well, I _____ (1. discuss) it with Mr Jones all morning. The guys down here _____ (2. strike) since last week. They _____ (3. complain) about pay and long working hours for some time now. However, he ensures me that he _____ (4. try) to sort this mess out. I _____ (5. see) this kind of situation before and we just have to be patient. Of course, it doesn't help that it _____ (6. rain) almost non-stop for the last five days. Still, the sun _____ (7. shine) all morning and I'm confident we can make some form of breakthrough here.

Arbeitsprozesse und laufende Tätigkeiten beschreiben

9. **Decide whether you should use simple present, present progressive, present perfect or present perfect progressive when you describe …**

a.	something that usually takes place.	simple present
b.	an action that has recently stopped.	
c.	something that's happening right now.	
d.	something that happened at an unspecified time in the past.	
e.	an action that has never taken place	
f.	something that is a fact.	
g.	the duration of an action that is ongoing.	
h.	an ongoing procedure.	

10. **Match the sentences below with the descriptions above.**

1.	The marketing manager has a large office.	f.
2.	I have been working on this report all morning.	
3.	They're conducting a lot of market research at the moment.	
4.	The conference calls generally take place first thing in the morning.	
5.	He's working closely with the customers on site.	
6.	Sales have been decreasing recently, but are now stable.	
7.	Demand has never been so high.	
8.	Don't worry, I've already spoken to Keith about this.	
9.	We're over budget on this project.	
10.	I'm currently interviewing new applicants for the internship.	
11.	The workers have already rejected the new payment conditions.	
12.	The workers have been striking for almost 36 hours now.	
13.	We normally have no problems with this construction company.	
14.	I've already found a potential new site in Ystad, in Sweden.	

Arbeitsprozesse und laufende Tätigkeiten beschreiben

11. Translate the following sentences into English using the present perfect.

Im Deutschen: Verb in der Gegenwart	Im Englischen: Verb im *present perfect* (*simple* oder *progressive*)
1. Ich **kenne** sie seit langer Zeit.	I've known her for a long time.
2. Sie **sind** seit vielen Jahren unsere besten Kunden.	
3. Er **hat** seit einer Woche ein Firmenauto.	
4. Wir **arbeiten** seit vielen Jahren zusammen.	
5. Herr Park **ist** seit sechs Jahren unserer Ansprechpartner in Korea.	
6. Ich **bin** seit zwei Jahren in der Marketingabteilung.	
7. Ich **spreche** seit drei Stunden mit Frau Wolf über die Kosten.	
8. Herr Bryant **ist** seit letzten Mai für die Bauarbeiten zuständig.	
9. Herr Jones **verhandelt** seit heute Morgen um 8 Uhr mit den Bauarbeitern.	
10. Die Firma **wartet** seit einigen Monaten auf diesen Geschäftsabschluss.	

Firmengeschichte und Produktentwicklungen präsentieren – Talking about the history of a company and the development of products

Simple past – past progressive *(while & when)* – past perfect – past perfect progressive

1. **Answer these questions by using your own ideas in the simple past.**

   1. When did you decide to move into a new building?

   _____
   _____

   2. Why did you choose this particular location?

   _____

   3. When did you last visit the construction site?

   _____

   4. How did the customers react to the building delays?

   _____
   _____

2. **Mr Bryant makes a speech at the groundbreaking ceremony. Tick the correct verb form.**

   "Ladies and gentleman, I just ☐ wanted / ☐ have wanted to say a few words. As many of you know, we ☐ had / ☐ have had a number of problems since we ☐ began / ☐ have begun construction almost one year ago. However, I'm pleased to say that the team of workers here ☐ did / ☐ have done a wonderful job to help us meet the deadline. And I'm sure that those of you who ☐ did go / ☐ have been inside already will agree that it ☐ was / ☐ has been worth the wait. When we ☐ signed / ☐ have signed the contract, fourteen months ago, we ☐ promised / ☐ have promised to deliver the most energy-efficient and technologically-advanced building around. And, ladies and gentleman, that is exactly what we ☐ did / ☐ have done. Before I finish, I'd also like to thank our man at the site, Mr Jones. As I ☐ said / ☐ have said a few moments ago, we ☐ had / ☐ have had our share of ups and downs over the last few months, and Mr Jones ☐ was / ☐ has been always the person who had to deal with them. So, a big thank you to him, to the workers, and everybody who ☐ was / ☐ has been involved so far, and who I ☐ forgot / ☐ have forgotten to thank."

Firmengeschichte und Produktentwicklungen präsentieren

3. **Use the words below to make sentences. Make sure you use the simple past and past perfect correctly.**

1. First they did a lot of market research. Then they released the *PC ToGo*.

   <u>After they had done a lot of market research, they</u>
   <u>released the PC ToGo. / Before they released the</u>
   <u>PC ToGo, they had done a lot of market research.</u>

2. The *PC ToGo* struggled against other handheld devices on the market. Then we added new applications.

3. We presented the product at the *e-urope* trade fair. Then interest increased.

4. We had a number of less successful models on the market. Then we launched the *PC ToGo*.

5. They had no success outside of Europe. Then they introduced the *PC ToGo*.

6. I didn't see the new features. Then I went to the *e-urope* event last month.

7. I had never been to a trade fair. Then I went to *e-urope*.

8. They showcased the product at *e-urope*. Did they test it before?

4. Mr Bryant is visiting Mr Jones at the construction site. He is unhappy with Mr Jones for a number of reasons. Put his reasons into the past perfect or the past perfect progressive.

1. You haven't contacted the customer yet.

2. The workers haven't been doing anything.

3. You haven't sent me regular updates, like I asked.

4. You haven't done what you promised you would.

5. You didn't tell me about the latest developments.

6. We haven't really made any progress.

7. The workers haven't started the repairs.

8. You haven't solved the problem with the roof.

Mr Bryant was angry with Mr Jones because …

1. he hadn't contacted the customers yet.
2. the workers
3.
4.
5.
6.
7.
8.

Firmengeschichte und Produktentwicklungen präsentieren

5. Use the words below to make sentences or questions in the past perfect or the past perfect progressive.

1. you / meet / the intern / before the office party?
   Had you met the intern before the office party?

2. she / talk / the architects / for hours / before they / reach / an agreement

3. the company / already / work / with the architects / on a previous project

4. I / see / the plans / before / he / call the meeting

5. the marketing team / have / meetings / for a long time / before the advertising campaign / finalised

6. they / interview / long / before they / suitable candidate / find?

6. Match the descriptions below with the correct tense.

a. describe an event that happened before another event in the past.	past progressive
b. describe two actions that were happening simultaneously in the past.	past perfect progressive
c. emphasize the duration of a completed action in the past.	simple past
d. something that happened at a fixed point in the past.	past perfect

Firmengeschichte und Produktentwicklungen präsentieren

7. Match the sentences with the descriptions from exercise 6 and come up with a sentence of your own in the same tense.

1. I hadn't been working on the project long when they pulled the plug. [c.]
   And now your own example …
   _____

2. I visited my first *e-urope* trade fair six years ago. [ ]
   And now your own example …
   _____

3. They only released the *PC ToGo* after they had carefully studied the competition and the market. [ ]
   And now your own example …
   _____

4. I was working in a different department when they asked me to join the marketing team. [ ]
   And now your own example …
   _____

5. After we had seen the new features, we knew it would be a success. [ ]
   And now your own example …
   _____

6. The construction work had only been going on for a few weeks when the problems began. [ ]
   And now your own example …
   _____

7. We discussed this with the client during our last meeting. [ ]
   And now your own example …
   _____

8. I was just writing you an email when you called. [ ]
   And now your own example …
   _____

Ziele und zukünftige Entwicklungen vorstellen – Presenting goals and future developments

Will-future

1. Answer the following questions.

1. – Will you still be here at 6 pm?

   – No, _____. I have to leave at 5.30 pm.

2. – Will Mr Williams be able to see me before his meeting this morning?

   – No, I'm afraid _____. I _____ make an appointment for you for this afternoon.

3. – Hi Laura. Will I see you at the meeting later?

   – Yes, _____. See you then.

4. – Will you and your team keep me updated with any developments?

   – Yes, of course _____.

5. – Kevin, when will I have your report on my desk?

   – _____ be finished by the end of the day.

"I think **I'm** free. **I'll** check my schedule."

2. Make will-future sentences or questions from these words. Use short forms where possible.

1. I / not be / in the office / tomorrow

   _____

2. I / be / at a conference / all day

   _____

3. when / you / be back / in the office / ?

   _____

4. I'm sure / they / be pleased / with the results

   _____

5. it / be ready / in time for the trade show / ?

   _____

6. I'm afraid / it / not be / ready on time

   _____

Going to-future

3. Congratulations! You have been promoted and are now head of the Stuttgart branch of *Howard Electronic Solutions*. The staff were not at all happy with the previous boss, and you are holding a speech to motivate them again. Use the notes to help you outline your intentions, and add a few of your own. Use the going to-future and write your speech on a separate sheet of paper.

- introduce flexible working hours
- increase holiday allowance by five days
- raise pay by ~~10%~~ 5%
- install suggestion box
- organize more company outings
- start a company ~~mud wrestling~~ football team
- ...

4. You have completed a research project for *Howard Electronic Solutions* and have made a number of predictions for the coming year. A meeting has been called for you to share your thoughts on what is going to happen. Make five more predictions.

Based on my research, I predict for the coming year ...

1. profits / by approximately 12.5% / rise

2. sales / by 2.2 million units / increase

3. competition / more aggressive / become

4. consumers / less money to spend / have

5. marketing / more important than ever / be

Ziele und zukünftige Entwicklungen vorstellen

Will-future vs. going to-future

5. Read the sentences from the meeting and tick the correct future form.

1. In my presentation, ☐ I'll / ☐ I'm going to outline our progress so far.
2. Do you have any new figures? ☐ I'll / ☐ I'm going to give Mr Williams an update this afternoon.
3. Can you hold on a second, ☐ I'll / ☐ I'm going to see if she is at her desk.
4. The deadline is approaching and we're understaffed. I can see already that ☐ we'll / ☐ we're going to struggle to meet the deadline.
5. Don't worry, I'm sure ☐ we'll / ☐ we're going to meet next month's deadline.
6. Can you let me know how you're getting on? – Of course, ☐ I'll / ☐ I'm going to call you early next week.
7. What time is the shipment arriving? – ☐ It'll / ☐ It's going to be here at 10 am.
8. I believe that this project ☐ will / ☐ is going to be a great success.

6. Read the following telephone conversation and complete the sentences using will-future or going to-future.

Good morning, James. Can I have a word with you this afternoon? It _____ (1. only take a few minutes).

Sure, _____ _____ (2. come to your office after lunch). How about 2 pm?

No, I'm afraid the IT technician _____ (3. be there then). How about 3 pm?

That's no good for me. I _____ (4. visit a client in the city) and I _____ (5. to leave at 2.45 pm). Plus, have you seen those black clouds? It's definitely _____ (6. to rain) and I'm sure the traffic _____ (7. be a nightmare!)

Ok, then we _____ (8. meet up in the morning) instead.

Great, I _____ (9. see you then).

Zukunftsformen im Überblick

7. Decide whether you should use will-future, going to-future, simple present or present progressive in the following situations.

a. a future plan	going to-future
b. an opinion about something in the future	
c. a prediction based on current evidence	
d. a fixed future arrangement	
e. a spontaneous decision	
f. a future fact	
g. timetables and schedules	
h. a confirmed activity in the future	

8. Match the sentences below with the uses from above.

1.	I think this will be a tough year for new companies.	b.
2.	Ms Moss won't be here next week. She'll be in Seoul.	
3.	I'm going to talk to the suppliers this afternoon.	
4.	The annual sales conference is in April this year.	
5.	The train leaves at 5.42 pm.	
6.	I'm meeting the potential investors next Monday.	
7.	With these rising costs it's going to be difficult to stay within the budget.	
8.	Thanks for the information. I'll pass it on to my supervisor right away.	

9. Read your horoscope for the day and write one for somebody you know well on an extra sheet of paper. Remember to use the will-future, and be creative!

Love: This will be an exciting month for your love life. The weekend will bring someone very special into your life who'll do anything to get your attention. But beware: jealous friends will do their best to keep you apart. ♥♥♥♥♥

Health: You will suffer from tiredness and a lack of enthusiasm. This will be especially bad on Monday mornings and will also affect many of your colleagues.

Job: Maybe you'll get a promotion, maybe you won't.

Money: Six numbers will bring you a lot of luck on Saturday – maybe.

Eigene Vorlieben und Stärken ausdrücken – Expressing personal preferences and strengths

Gerundium & Infinitiv – Gerund vs. infinitive

1. Complete this dialogue from a job interview using either gerund or infinitive.

   – So Mr Bauer, would you mind _____ (1. tell) us a little bit about yourself?

   – Of course. As you can see on my CV, I recently finished _____ (2. study) electrical engineering at university in Cologne. After graduation I considered _____ (3. continue) my studies, but then I decided _____ (4. look) for a job instead.

   – And why did you decide _____ (5. do) that? Won't you miss _____ (6. study)?

   – I don't think so. In fact, I hope _____ (7. continue) while I work. And this was the main reason I chose _____ (8. apply) at this company.

   – Well, we hope that all of our employees continue _____ (9. learn) while they are with us. Tell me, Mr Bauer. What are your strengths? What qualities do you have? What do you like _____ (10. do) in your free time?

2. Translate the following sentences using either gerund or infinitive. Use the words in brackets.

   1. Denken Sie daran, die E-Mail anzuhängen. (remember)

   2. Können Sie sich vorstellen, von zu Hause zu arbeiten? (imagine)

   3. Es macht mir nichts aus, heute länger zu arbeiten. (mind)

   4. Wir müssen es vermeiden, das Budget zu überschreiten. (avoid)

   5. Ich muss mit dem Kunden darüber sprechen. (need)

   6. Ich rechne damit, bald Fortschritte zu sehen. (expect)

Eigene Vorlieben und Stärken ausdrücken

3. Rewrite the following sentences using either gerund or infinitive.

1. Ruben: "Don't worry. I will finish the sales figures by 5 pm."
   <u>Ruben promised **to finish** the sales figures by 5 pm.</u>

2. Caroline: "I like Jacob, but I work better with Max."
   <u>Caroline likes Jacob, but prefers</u>

3. Peter: "Why don't you try different software?"
   <u>Peter suggested</u>

4. Emma: "Can I give you a lift to the airport, James?"
   <u>Emma offered</u>

5. Claire: "I think I'm going to talk to my boss."
   <u>Claire considered</u>

6. Matt: "I started this project three weeks ago."
   <u>Matt began</u>

7. Judith: "Can we get together at 3.30 pm in my office, Michael?"
   Michael: "Yes, that's fine."
   <u>Judith and Michael arranged</u>

8. Matt: "Marianne, can you help me with my presentation this afternoon?"
   Marianne: "Yes, of course."
   <u>Marianne agreed</u>

9. Tom: "Good morning, Daniel. Did you bring that report for me?"
   Daniel: "I'm very sorry but I forgot."
   <u>Daniel forgot</u>

10. Peter: "Hi James. I called you earlier, but you weren't at your desk."
    <u>Peter tried</u>

4. Imagine you are at the interview from exercise 1. Use both gerund and infinitive to write a list of your strengths, qualities and free-time activities. Use a separate sheet of paper.

I'm good at ...
I like ...
I enjoy ...
I'm able ...
In my free time, I ...
...

Produkte und Dienstleistungen beschreiben – Describing products and services

Steigerung der Adjektive – Comparison of adjectives

1. The next day you are talking about the trade fair in class. One of your classmates is telling a story about two salespeople from different companies. Complete what she said using comparatives of adjectives.

> … you should have heard it! They both represented companies that sold handheld computers. The woman's company was promoting the *PC ToGo* and the man's company the *Hand-e*.

When she said …

1. "Our product is brand new on the market."
2. "As you can see, the *PC ToGo* has a large display."
3. "The *PC ToGo*'s design is very modern."
4. "The technology behind the *PC ToGo* is incredibly advanced."
5. "But it is not only about technology. The design is extremely elegant and beautiful."
6. "What's more, the *PC ToGo* is equipped with a large memory."
7. "And of course, the price is low."

… then he said …

1. *"Our product is even newer."*
2. _____
3. _____
4. _____
5. _____
6. _____
7. _____

Produkte und Dienstleistungen beschreiben

2. Below are the descriptions of the two handheld computers. Use the information in the table to make six sentences to compare the products. Use the comparative of the adjective and *than*.

PC ToGo		Hand-e	
Memory:	128 MB	**Memory:**	64 MB
Screen:	3.7 inches	**Screen:**	3.4 inches
Battery life:	12 hours	**Battery life:**	8 hours
Features:	USB, Wi-Fi, MP3, Camera, Bluetooth, Video, FM radio	**Features:**	USB, Wi-Fi, MP3, Camera, Video, FM radio
Height:	4.5 inches	**Height:**	4.3 inches
Width:	2.9 inches	**Width:**	3.2 inches
Weight:	100 g	**Weight:**	125 g
Warranty:	12 months	**Warranty:**	3 months
Price:	$389	**Price:**	$249

1. *The PC ToGo is lighter than the Hand-e.*
2.
3.
4.
5.
6.
7.

Adjektive & Adverbien – Adjectives vs. adverbs

3. **Adjective or adverb?** *Bits & Bytes,* a leading technology magazine, has written a review of the *PC ToGo.* Tick the correct box.

Due to its ☐ high / ☐ highly speed processor, the *PC ToGo* is able to download information ☐ quick / ☐ quickly and ☐ easy / ☐ easily from the Web. The 3.7 inch ☐ large / ☐ largely screen offers an ☐ excellent / ☐ excellently picture quality as well as ☐ smooth / ☐ smoothly running videos.
The 128 MB memory means the *PC ToGo* has a ☐ large / ☐ largely storage capacity and the ☐ powerful / ☐ powerfully battery makes it the perfect companion for long-haul flights.
What's more, its slim and ☐ beautiful / ☐ beautifully design means that it not only fits ☐ perfect / ☐ perfectly into your pocket, but it will also make all your friends and colleagues jealous.
In conclusion, although it is quite ☐ expensive / ☐ expensively we believe that the *PC ToGo* is a ☐ good / ☐ well investment for anybody that wants to take their business with them. Go on, treat yourself!

Star rating: ★ ★ ★ ★ ★

Steigerung der Adverbien – Comparison of adverbs

4. Complete the table below to test your knowledge.

	adverb	comparative	superlative	adjective
1.				good
2.		more regularly		
3.	effectively			
4.			easiest	
5.	recently			
6.				efficient
7.		more slowly		
8.			fastest	
9.				careful
10.	badly			

Produkte und Dienstleistungen beschreiben

5. **The CEO of *Future Tech*, the company which manufactures the *Hand-e*, also visited the trade fair and has called a meeting to give her staff some feedback. Use the comparative of the adverb on the right to rewrite the sentences.**

1. The battery takes too long to recharge.
   The battery must recharge more quickly.   (quickly)

2. Sales of the *Hand-e* have been too low.
   It must sell   (well)

3. Our marketing campaign is not very effective.
   We must market   (effectively)

4. I don't think we are working hard enough.
   We have to work   (hard)

5. I'm afraid your presentation was not very clear.
   You should present   (clearly)

6. I didn't understand everything. You spoke too fast.
   Why don't you   (slowly)

6. **After another trade fair one year later, the CEO of *Future Tech* called a meeting to tell her team how pleased she was with the improvements she had seen. Take her role and praise your team, using the superlative form of the adverbs in brackets.**

1. Our product has sold the best!   (our product – sell – well)
2. _____   (you – work – hard)
3. _____   (we – improve – much)
4. _____   (our profits – rise – fast)
5. _____   (we – market – effectively)
6. _____   (our customers – complain – little)

Abläufe in Einzelheiten darstellen – Describing procedures in detail

Relativsätze – Relative clauses

1. **Complete the sentences below by inserting either *who, which* or *that*.**

   1. The secretary, _____ is writing an email, wants to inform everybody about the meeting.
   2. The company _____ is looking for a new intern has a very young workforce.
   3. The conference room, _____ is on the fourth floor, is closed for refurbishments.
   4. The IT technician _____ is coming in this afternoon can fix anything.
   5. The team _____ are working on the new project are under a lot of pressure.
   6. The new project, _____ is for the Asian market, is worth a lot of money.
   7. My friend, _____ works in recruiting, says that this is a good time to be looking for a job.
   8. The applicant _____ was here this morning had very impressive references.
   9. My previous position, _____ was with a small translation company, taught me how to work under pressure.
   10. Both interns _____ started last year have been employed on a permanent basis.

2. **Dominique, one of the HR managers at *Sports Island*, explains what she looks for in an applicant. Fill in the gaps using either *who, which, that* or *whose*.**

   As a company _____ (1.) works in an international market, we're always on the lookout for people _____ (2.) speak good English. However, that doesn't mean that an applicant _____ (3.) native language is English is guaranteed a job. We're interested in people _____ (4.) are young, dynamic, and _____ (5.) are motivated. We want people _____ (6.) interests and goals match those of *Sports Island*. And of course, someone _____ (7.) experience and qualifications are first class will almost certainly be invited for an interview. And when they come in, first impressions count. We want people _____ (8.) are punctual, polite, and people _____ (9.) can show us that they really want to work here.

3. **Two young professionals are giving their opinions on finding the right job. Fill in the gaps using either *who, which, that* or *whose*.**

My friend, _____ (1.) is a software designer, swears by social networking sites. But I don't like the idea of having my details on a site _____ (2.) anybody can look at!

Ask, ask, ask. If you know someone _____ (3.) you think can help you, talk to them. Maybe you have a friend _____ (4.) father, mother, or brother has a high position in a company. After all, it's not what you know, it's who you know.

4. **With or without commas? Look at the sentences below and decide if and where you need to insert a comma.**

1. Companies that offer their employees good chances for advancement are very attractive.
2. My friend who I studied with in Hamburg used to work in the HR department and has put in a good word for me.
3. Laura whose brother completed an internship here last year works in our purchasing department.
4. Is Douglas the person who interviewed you for your internship?
5. *Fit4Life* who are one of the leading sports companies in Europe have also offered me a position.
6. I'm looking for a job that involves international travel opportunities.

5. **Use a non-defining relative clause to make two sentences into one. Decide whether you need to use *who, which* or *whose*. Write on an extra sheet of paper.**

1. The new job advertisement has had a lot of response. We posted it on *joblink.com*.
2. The upcoming job fair will be a good opportunity to meet prospective employers. The job fair will be in Brighton this year.
3. The research and development team are looking for a new intern. They have just started on a new project.
4. The next applicant is coming in at 11 am for her interview. Her name is Elisabeth Preston.
5. The social networking site *joblink.com* is a great place to look for internships and full-time positions. The site has over 650,000 members.

Anleitungen und Rat geben – Giving instructions and advice

Modalverben – Modal verbs

1. **John and Tim are continuing their conversation. Fill in *can, may, should, must, needn't* or *mustn't*. For some sentences, more than one solution is possible.**

   1. You _____ call if you are running late. But you _____ worry if it is only five minutes.
   2. _____ I use the Internet to check my emails?
   3. Of course. However, you _____ only do this during your breaks.
   4. You _____ discuss confidential information outside of the office. This is very important.
   5. You _____ use the company gym, but you _____ register first.
   6. You _____ always make sure your workspace is tidy at the end of the day.
   7. Who _____ I talk to if I am having problems?
   8. Good question. If you are having difficulties with anything, then you _____ talk to Julia, your team leader.
   9. On your first day, you _____ sign in at reception. But once you have your ID card, you _____ bother.
   10. I'm going to write this down. I _____ forget anything.

2. **Tim is telling John about his internship last summer. Fill in the missing parts of the conversation using substitutes for modals in the simple past.**

   John: It says in your CV that you _____ (1. must) complete an internship as part of your degree last year. Can you tell me a little bit about that?

   Tim: Certainly. Well, it was quite an experience. It was at a small advertising agency in my town. I chose it because it was close by and I _____ (2. can) get there on foot.

   John: What _____ (3. must) do there?

   Tim: Firstly, every morning I _____ (4. must) make coffee for the boss. I _____ (5. mustn't) start my own work before it was made.

Anleitungen und Rat geben

John: Well that's something I haven't heard before!

Tim: That wasn't the only thing. In the beginning, I _____ (6. must) ask to go to the toilet.

John: You _____ (7. may not) go to the toilet without asking?

Tim: I know! It is unbelievable. Also, workers _____ (8. may) smoke in the office. I _____ (9. can't) work with all that smoke.

John: Were there any positive things about the job?

Tim: Yes. I _____ (10. needn't) work late very often, but I _____ (11. mustn't) leave early on Fridays.

3. John is telling Tim what he can expect from his new position at *Sports Island*. Fill in the missing parts of the conversation using the substitute for modals in will-future.

1. We have a lot of projects at the moment, so you _____ (must) work late sometimes.
2. However, often you _____ (may) leave early on Fridays.
3. You _____ (can't) access the company intranet for the first few days. We _____ (must) get you a username and a password first.
4. Unfortunately, you _____ (mustn't) make use of the company discount card until you have been here for three months. It's just the company policy, I'm afraid.
5. However, you _____ (can) sign up for free language classes.
6. And don't worry, here you _____ (needn't) make coffee for the boss.

4. Today is the first day of your internship at *Sports Island*. You are meeting John Fisher in the canteen. Use an extra sheet of paper.

a. Fragen Sie ihn, …

1. … ob man in der Kantine rauchen darf,
2. … ob man den firmeneigenen Laptop mit nach Hause nehmen darf,
3. … wie lange man freitags arbeiten muss,
4. … ob Sie immer einen Anzug / ein Kostüm tragen müssen,
5. … ob Sie sich den anderen Kollegen vorstellen sollten.

b. Wie könnten Johns Antworten auf die Fragen lauten?

1. <u>No, you can't smoke in the canteen. You have to use the special smoking areas on each floor.</u>
2. …

Erfolgreich über Bedingungen verhandeln – Negotiating terms and conditions successfully

If-Sätze, Typ I – If-clauses, type I

1. **Use the words to make positive statements with if-clauses, type I.**

   1. you / buy from us / be satisfied
      <u>If you buy from us, you will be satisfied.</u>

   2. you / find a better price / we / match it
      _____

   3. we / make this deal / Mr Fisher / be very happy
      _____

   4. you / pay in cash / I / lower the price
      _____

   5. she / get the job / move to San Francisco
      _____

   "I'll give in **if** you do."

2. **Two colleagues are about to go into a meeting to negotiate a large contract. Complete their conversation.**

   - Ok, this is serious. If we _____ (1. not get) a good price, we _____ (2. not stay) on budget.

   - You're right. But if we _____ (3. offer) too little, they _____ (4. not take) us seriously. And if they _____ (5. not take) us seriously, we _____ (6. not have) a chance.

   - I reckon we _____ (7. have) a better chance if we _____ (8. not look) nervous.

   - Ok, I _____ (9. stay) cool if you _____ (10. do).

   - That's easier said than done. Ms Sherman is expecting a result. She _____ (11. not be) very happy if we _____ (12. come) home empty handed.

   - Yeah, you're right. In fact, I think that if we _____ (13. not win) this contract, we _____ (14. be) looking for a new job in the near future.

If-Sätze, Typ II – If-clauses, type II

3. Translate the if-clauses, type II sentences into English.

1. An Ihrer Stelle würde ich das Eröffnungsangebot überdenken.

___

2. Wenn Sie das neue Modell sehen würden, wären Sie begeistert.

___

3. Wenn unsere Firmen eine Partnerschaft eingehen würden, wäre es für beide Seiten vorteilhaft.

___

4. Wir würden auf das Geschäft eingehen, wenn ihr Angebot nicht unser Budget überschreiten würde.

___

5. Würden Sie es in Betracht ziehen, wenn wir den Preis um 5% reduzieren würden?

___

6. Wenn wir ihnen eine kostenlose Lieferung der Teile anbieten würden, würden sie das Angebot vielleicht akzeptieren.

___

4. Fill in the gaps using either if-clauses, type I or type II.

- Are you interested in the *Hand-e*, sir?
- I _____ (1.) be if you reduced the price.
- If I could, I _____ (2.). But unfortunately, that isn't possible.
- It's a lot of money. What happens if something _____ (3.) wrong?
- That's no problem. If you _____ (4.) the *Hand-e* from us, you'll receive a 90 day guarantee. So if you _____ (5.) unsatisfied for any reason, you will receive a full refund.
- That means that if I _____ (6.) unsatisfied with the phone, I could get my money back?
- Precisely. And, if you _____ (7.) cash, I'll throw in an in-car kit free of charge. So, shall I prepare the paperwork?
- No, I'm sorry. I think I'll leave it. But if I change mind, I _____ (8.) come back.

Erfolgreich über Bedingungen verhandeln

5. Rewrite the sentences to form negative statements.

1. Michael has a lot of negotiating experience. He doesn't get nervous.
   <u>If Michael didn't have a lot of negotiating experience, he would get nervous.</u>

2. Sally is well prepared. She has a good chance of making a deal.

3. Matthew speaks three languages. He is often chosen to represent the company at trade fairs.

4. Erkan makes a lot of profit every year. He is the company's top salesman.

6. Two colleagues are chatting over lunch. Use their answers to write the questions using if-clauses, type II.

1. _____

Oh, let me see. If I could live anywhere, I would live in Italy, in Florence.

Good question! I think that if I didn't have to work, I would try to write a crime novel.

2. _____

3. _____

That's easy. If I could have anybody's office, I would have yours. That view is amazing!

If-Sätze, Typ III – If-clauses, type III

7. Use the following negative statements to make positive statements.

1. They didn't offer me enough money. I didn't accept their offer.
   If they had offered me enough money, I would have accepted their offer.

2. Mr Cohen's presentation didn't convince me. I didn't go ahead with the project.

3. Ms Saunders wasn't a confident negotiator. We didn't achieve our target price.

4. Your company's order wasn't large enough. We couldn't give you a discount.

5. I didn't agree with the terms. I didn't sign the contract.

8. Read the email from Ms Wolf, in reference to her negotiations with Mr Perry, and write what would have happened if things had been different.

Re: Negotiations with Mr Perry
Dear Mr Sherman, I have just returned from my meeting with Mr Perry. I'm afraid we will have to consider other suppliers for the Riverside project. Mr Perry and I were unable to come to an agreement for the following reasons: – he was not prepared to negotiate, – his company could not guarantee delivery by the end of the month, – he didn't have an up-to-date price list with him, – his company's delivery policy was not clear, – he has no experience of working on large projects, – his company wasn't able to fill our order. Regards, C. Wolf

They might have come to an agreement if …

1. *he had been prepared to negotiate,*
2.
3.
4.
5.
6.

Erfolgreich über Bedingungen verhandeln

9. Complete this table by inserting the appropriate if-clauses.

If-clause, type I	If-clause, type II	If-clause, type III
If you include delivery, we will sign the contract.	If you included delivery, we would sign the contract.	If you had included delivery, we would have signed the contract.
If you order 100 units, the company will give you a 10% discount.		
	If they hired Robin, he would do a great job.	
		If it had been my decision, I would have accepted their offer.
The company will be in trouble if the new range of products doesn't sell well.		
	I would do the negotiations myself if I wasn't too busy.	
		We wouldn't have needed to extend the deadline if we had had good weather.
Will you be available if I need you?		
	Would you consider their offer if they lowered the price a little?	
		What would have happened if we hadn't met the deadline?

Prozesse und Maschinen beschreiben

9. **Rewrite the reporter's questions in the passive voice.**

   1. "When did you introduce the new machines?"
      When were the new machines introduced?
   2. "Can you now produce more components in a shorter time?"

   _____

   3. "Have you trained all of your employees on the new machines?"

   _____

   4. "Will you need to increase your workforce to cope with the increased production?"

   _____

   5. "In how many of your factories are you using these machines?"

   _____

10. Use Mr Franklin's answers to write a short newspaper article, reporting on the changes at *Howard Electronic Solutions*. Use the passive voice in as many tenses as possible. The headline and the introduction have already been done for you.

    1. "We started using the machines two weeks ago."
    2. "Yes, these new machines have greatly improved our production capabilities."
    3. "Not yet. So far, we've only trained our most experienced employees on the new machines. However, we will train all factory workers by the end of this month."
    4. "We're not sure whether or not we'll have to increase our staff."
    5. "We are using these new machines in over half of our factories, and we hope to install them in all sites by the end of the year."

    ***Howard Electronic Solutions* double production capabilities**

    Thanks to some innovative new machinery, *Howard Electronic Solutions* is looking to become a market leader. The new machines started being used two weeks ago and production capabilities …

Prozesse und Maschinen beschreiben

6. Rewrite the following sentences in the passive form.

1. *Howard Electronic Solutions* has ordered some more components.
   Some more components ... _____

2. Emma has confirmed the visit of Mr Park tomorrow.
   _____

3. Julian has informed the factory staff about Mr Park's visit.
   _____

4. Have you made the itinerary for his visit yet?
   _____

5. I haven't planned the itinerary for his visit yet.
   _____

7. Below is Julian's checklist for Mr Park's visit. What has or hasn't been done?

- clean office ✓
- service machines ✓
- organise tour ✓
- arrange lunch
- prepare speech ✓
- speak to Mr Franklin

1. The office has been cleaned.
2. The machines _____
3. _____
4. _____
5. _____
6. _____

8. Rewrite the questions and answers below using the passive voice.

1. Yes, the staff _____

Has Julian trained the staff on the machines yet?

2. Have the machines _____?

Yes, Tom and Sarah cleaned them this morning.

3. No, the _____

Have we filled the order yet?

Über Ereignisse im Unternehmen berichten – Reporting about events in the company

Indirekte Rede – Reported speech

1. During your internship at *Sports Island*, the CEO gives his annual report on what has happened over the last 12 months. Your supervisor is unable to attend the meeting and has sent you in her place. You report back to her the following day.

1. The company has recorded its highest profit for three years.

2. This has been a successful year for the company.

3. Our latest range of products is outselling the competition by two to one.

4. The company are currently working on an exciting new project.

5. Does anybody have anything to add?

6. I believe there will be many new challenges next year.

1. He said _____

2. He mentioned _____

3. He claimed _____

4. He told us _____

5. He asked _____

6. He finished by saying _____

Über Ereignisse im Unternehmen berichten

2. Put these questions into reported speech.

1. Are you coming to the pub after work?
2. What do you think about the new design?
3. How long has the new model been on the market for?
4. Did you go to the CEO's meeting yesterday?
5. What are you working on at the moment?
6. Can you give me a progress report this afternoon?

1. He asked if _____
2. _____
3. _____
4. _____
5. _____
6. _____

3. These sentences are already in reported speech. Put them back into direct speech. Use short forms as much as possible.

1. He said that the conference call with the customers was taking place at 2.45 pm, in room 1.43.

2. She said she didn't think that she would be able to make it.

3. She wanted to know if they thought the new range of products would be a success.

4. They said that they were sure the new range of products would be a great success.

5. He said that he'd been working on the new designs all morning.

6. He wanted to know what the new intern's name was.

7. She asked how long I had worked for the company.

8. I told him I'd been working here since last September.

Prozesse und Maschinen beschreiben – Describing processes and machines

Passiv – Passive voice

1. Use the following words to make passive sentences.

1. machines / service / once a month
   The machines are serviced once a month.

2. all components / make / in this factory
   _____

3. most workers / train / on this machine
   _____

4. the components / ship / all around the world
   _____

5. spare parts for the machine / deliver / from Stuttgart
   _____

6. our IT system / update / every two years
   _____

7. the old machines / not use / very often
   _____

8. the holes / not drill / manually anymore
   _____

2. Translate the following questions into English using the passive.

- Sind alle Arbeiter in der Benutzung der Maschinen geschult worden?

  1. _____

- Wie viele Komponenten werden pro Tag hergestellt?

  2. _____

- Wie oft wird die Maschine auf Fehler überprüft?

  3. _____

Prozesse und Maschinen beschreiben

3. Read what Julian is saying and underline the passive constructions.

When the new machines <u>were delivered</u>, I was given the responsibility for training the rest of the workers down here in the factory. I was asked by Mr Franklin, the Head of Production to take small teams and familiarise them with the new process. The training lasted one day, and a new team were sent to me every morning. It was hard work but I'm happy that I was given the opportunity to share my skills and experience with others. Mr Franklin told me I had done a good job. In fact, he offered me a promotion. You're now talking to the factory supervisor.

4. Find the two active constructions in the text and rewrite them using the passive.

1. _____
2. _____

5. Julian talks more about his job offer from Mr Franklin. Write the sentences in the passive.

1. "Mr Franklin offered me more responsibility."

   Julian was promised _____

2. "Mr Franklin gave me a company laptop."

   _____

3. "He promised me a pay rise and an office on the factory floor."

   _____

   _____

4. "But he warned me about the longer hours."

   _____

   _____

5. "And, he told me not to plan any holidays in the near future."

   _____

   _____